MISSISSIPPI

MISSISSIPPI

HELLO
U.S.A.

by Anna Ready

Lerner Publications Company

You'll find this picture of a cotton plant at the beginning of each chapter in this book. Mississippi farmers have been growing cotton for hundreds of years. It is still one of the state's most valuable crops. It is used mainly to make clothing. Cotton grows well in Mississippi because of the state's warm climate and rich soil.

Cover (left): A paddlewheel boat docks at Natchez, Mississippi. Cover (right): Members of a marching band at a political rally. Pages 2–3: Stanton Hall, a mansion in Natchez, Mississippi. Page 3: A magnolia blossom.

This book is available in two editions:
Library binding by Lerner Publications Company, a division of Lerner Publishing Group
Soft cover by First Avenue Editions, an imprint of Lerner Publishing Group
241 First Avenue North
Minneapolis, MN 55401 U.S.A.

Website address: www.lernerbooks.com

Library of Congress Cataloging-in-Publication Data

Ready, Anna.
    Mississippi / by Anna Ready.— Rev. and expanded 2nd edition.
       p.   cm. — (Hello U.S.A.)
    Includes index.
    Summary: Introduces the geography, history, people, and environmental issues of Mississippi.
       ISBN: 0–8225–4109–2 (lib. bdg. : alk. paper)
       ISBN: 0–8225–0784–6 (pbk. : alk. paper)
       1. Mississippi—Juvenile literature. [1. Mississippi.] I. Title. II. Series.
    F341.3 .R43 2003
    976.2—dc21   2002008895

Manufactured in the United States of America
1 2 3 4 5 6 – JR – 08 07 06 05 04 03

CONTENTS

Bluffs tower over the broad Mississippi River near Natchez, Mississippi.

THE LAND

The Magnolia State

 ississippi's nickname, the Magnolia State, comes from a beautiful evergreen tree with sweet-smelling white flowers. Magnolias grow throughout Mississippi. The state boasts many other kinds of natural beauty, ranging from lush forests to white, sandy beaches to the wide waters of the Mississippi River, the river from which the state takes its name.

Mississippi is a southern state. Its neighbors are Tennessee, Alabama, Louisiana, and Arkansas. The Mississippi River, which empties into the Gulf of Mexico, forms most of the state's western border. The Gulf of Mexico, part of the Atlantic Ocean, washes up against Mississippi's southern coast. A series of small islands, together called the Gulf Islands National Seashore, lies just off the shore.

N
W · E
S

MISSISSIPPI
Political Map

★ State capital

0   20   40 Miles
0   20   40   60   80 Kilometers

Clarksdale ●

● Oxford

● Tupelo

Vardaman ●

Aberdeen ●

Greenwood ●

Columbus ●

Greenville ●

Belzoni ●

Tinsley ●

Philadelphia ●

Canton ●

Flora ●

Meridian ●

★ Jackson

Vicksburg ●

Mize ●

Fayette ●

Natchez ●

Hattiesburg ● ● Petal

The drawing of Mississippi on this page is called a political map. It shows features created by people, including cities and parks. The map on the facing page is called a physical map. It shows physical features of Mississippi, such as coasts, islands, hills, and rivers. The colors represent a range of elevations, or heights above sea level (see legend box). This map also shows the geographical regions of Mississippi.

Gulfport ●

● Biloxi

● Pascagoula

Gulf Islands
National Seashore

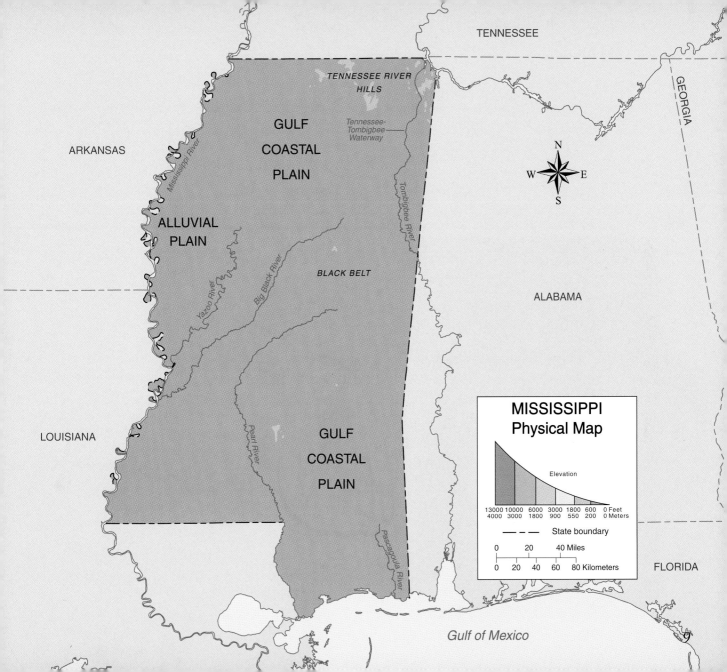

TENNESSEE

TENNESSEE RIVER HILLS

GULF

COASTAL

PLAIN

Tennessee-
Tombigbee
Waterway

ARKANSAS

Mississippi River

GEORGIA

ALLUVIAL

PLAIN

Tombigbee River

BLACK BELT

ALABAMA

Yazoo River

Big Black River

LOUISIANA

Pearl River

GULF

COASTAL

PLAIN

N
W   E
S

MISSISSIPPI
Physical Map

Elevation

| 13000 | 10000 | 6000 | 3000 | 1800 | 600 | 0 Feet |
| 4000 | 3000 | 1800 | 900 | 550 | 200 | 0 Meters |

- - - State boundary

0   20   40 Miles

0   20   40   60   80 Kilometers

Pascagoula River

FLORIDA

Gulf of Mexico

9

Mississippi is divided into two main regions. The Alluvial Plain is the name for a narrow strip of land along the western edge of the state. The soil of the plain, called **alluvium**, is a fertile mixture of fine dirt, clay, sand, and gravel. This rich soil has built up over the years as rivers have flooded their banks.

The area of soil enriched by flooding is known as a **delta.** In fact, most Mississippians refer to the Alluvial Plain as the Delta. Cotton and soybeans grow very well here.

The other main region, the Gulf Coastal Plain, extends from the Delta to the eastern edge of the state. The

The sun sets over the Mississippi Delta.

Loblolly and other kinds of pine trees thrive in the Piney Woods.

Piney Woods are located at the southern end of this plain. These woods are home to loblolly, long-leaf, and slash pine trees. The coastal plain also contains lowlands and **prairies**, or grasslands. Farmers grow corn and hay in the rich, dark soil of the Black Belt, the region's largest prairie. Cattle graze on the Black Belt's grasses.

   Mississippi's land slopes gently downward from its highest point in the north to sea level at the Gulf of Mexico. The Tennessee River Hills rise in the northeastern corner of the state. The tallest of these hills reaches 806 feet. It is the highest point in Mississippi.

Colorful bluffs rise near a river in southeastern Mississippi.

In winter Mississippi is home to Canada geese.

The Mississippi River is the state's most important waterway. In fact, Mississippi means "great water" or "big river" in the language of the American Indians who lived near the river long ago.

Smaller rivers such as the Big Black and the Yazoo flow westward into the Mississippi. The Pearl, Pascagoula, and Tombigbee Rivers flow into the Gulf of Mexico.

Mississippi's climate is warm and moist. The average rainfall in the north is more than 50 inches a year. Even more rain falls in the southeastern part of the state near the Gulf of Mexico. Occasionally, northern Mississippians see snow fall in their region, but the snow usually melts quickly.

Winter days in Mississippi are often foggy and damp.

The warm Mississippi winter brings only occasional snow and ice.

Winters are short and mild, with average temperatures of about 46° F. Mississippi's summers are long and often hot. Winds from the Gulf of Mexico cool the state in the summertime, when the average temperature is about 81° F. However, in some parts of the state, summer temperatures can sometimes reach 90° F.

During the late summer and early fall, violent storms called hurricanes sometimes blow in from the Gulf of Mexico. The storms' heavy rains, high waves, and strong winds can cause serious damage to towns along the coast.

Mississippi's state flower is the magnolia.

Flowering shrubs grow well in Mississippi's rich soil and warm, wet climate. Azaleas, camellias, and dogwoods grow throughout the state. More than 100 kinds of trees grow in the state's forests, including magnolia, pecan, palm, cottonwood, tupelo, oak, and pine trees. Woodlands cover nearly two-thirds of the state.

Mississippi's forests are home to many animals, including deer, foxes, opossums, rabbits, squirrels, quail, and wild turkeys. An adventurous hiker walking through the woods might spot an alligator swimming in a pond. Anglers catch bass, bream, and catfish in the state's many rivers. In the waters of the Gulf of Mexico, fishers haul in shrimp, crabs, and oysters.

Alligators *(above)* and box turtles *(right)* are among the state's many animal residents.

THE HISTORY

Cultural Crossroads

housands of years ago, no one lived in the region that would later become Mississippi. Its land was rich and forested. Far to the north, near the Arctic Ocean, an icy land bridge stretched between Asia and North America.

More than 20,000 years ago, hunters from Asia followed wild animals across the land bridge. As thousands of years passed, groups of people migrated, or traveled, farther and farther south. They arrived in the region that would later become the United States. These people are called Native Americans, or American Indians.

Ancient Indian mounds are still visible in many parts of the state. Some of the mounds were built as burial sites.

By A.D. 700, some Native Americans had reached the Mississippi region. These early inhabitants of Mississippi buried their dead in big pits. They piled dirt on top of the pits to form giant mounds.

Priests and chiefs lived on special mounds built just for them. Villagers lived in houses near the mounds. Historians refer to this group of Native Americans as mound builders.

By A.D. 1500, most of the mound builders had disappeared. No one knows what happened to them. By then, other Indian groups—the Natchez, Choctaw, and Chickasaw—had settled in villages on the eastern banks of the Mississippi River. These groups were probably related to the mound builders. Many smaller Indian groups also lived nearby.

Native Americans used some burial mounds as places of worship.

Lacrosse was a popular sport played by the Choctaw and other Indian groups.

The largest and most powerful group, or nation, was the Natchez, who lived in southwestern Mississippi. The Natchez were skilled at making cloth and pottery. For food, the Natchez planted corn, melons, squash, and beans. They hunted deer and caught fish. Like their ancestors, they also built mounds.

The Natchez divided their society into different levels. At the top was the king, called the Great Sun, and his family. At the bottom were common people, called Stinkards, who did the hard work of farming and mound building.

The Choctaw lived in the south-central part of Mississippi. They planted crops and built canoes, which they used for fishing, hunting, and trading trips. The Choctaw, like many other Indian nations, played lacrosse, a game played with special rackets and a ball.

The Chickasaw lived in villages in northern Mississippi. Each Chickasaw village was run by a chief. Like the Choctaw and the Natchez, the Chickasaw farmed and fished for food. They also raised cattle.

Hernando de Soto was the first European to explore Mississippi.

By the 1540s, between 25,000 and 35,000 American Indians were living in what later became Mississippi. At that time, Europeans began to visit the area. Searching for gold, Spanish explorer Hernando de Soto and his army passed through Chickasaw territory. De Soto demanded that the Indians carry supplies for his men.

The Chickasaw refused to obey the Spaniards. In the battle that followed, many Native Americans and several Spaniards were killed. De Soto and his army left the area without finding gold.

Mississippi's Indians did not see another European person until 1682, when French explorer René-Robert Cavelier de La Salle arrived in the area.

René-Robert Cavelier de La Salle claimed the entire Mississippi River valley for France.

La Salle traveled down the Mississippi River from Illinois to the Gulf of Mexico. He claimed the river's valley—including what later became Mississippi—for France. The explorer named the region Louisiana, after Louis XIV, the king of France.

Soon, more Europeans began to arrive in Mississippi. In 1698 British traders came to the area. By 1716 the French had established two settlements in the region—one near Biloxi and the other at Natchez. The British and the French traded cloth, guns, beads, and knives with the Indians in exchange for animal furs. The furs were then sold in Europe for a huge profit.

Both France and Great Britain claimed a lot of land in North America. The more land they had, the more money they could make from furs and other natural resources. Between 1754 and 1763, the two nations fought over who would claim the

In the early 1700s, the French shipped people from West Africa to what later became Mississippi. The Africans were forced to work as slaves on rice and tobacco farms.

most land in North America.

During this conflict—known as the French and Indian War—the Choctaw sided with the French, and the Chickasaw sided with the British. Great Britain won the war, gaining control of most of France's land in North America, including Mississippi.

But British rule did not last long. From 1775 to 1783, American colonists fought for independence from Great Britain. They defeated the British and formed a new nation, the United States of America.

The Natchez helped the French build Fort Rosalie, but later they attacked it.

The Natchez Revolt

The French were the first Europeans that settled in Mississippi. They built several settlements along the Mississippi River in southwestern Mississippi. At first, the French got along well with the American Indians living in the area. In 1716 Natchez Indians even helped the French build Fort Rosalie, a trading post and fort overlooking the Mississippi near modern-day Natchez.

But as more French settlers came to the area, they gradually claimed more and more of the fertile land that belonged to the Natchez. In 1729 the French governor of the Mississippi River valley decided to build a large farm on the site of a major Natchez Indian village. He ordered all the Indians to leave at once.

But the Natchez did not want to lose any more of their land. They decided to fight for their village and attacked Fort Rosalie and other French settlements along the river. The French army struck back and by 1731 had killed almost every member of the Natchez nation. The few surviving Indians either settled with other groups in the region or were sold into slavery. With this conflict, which was called the Natchez Revolt, the Natchez people were destroyed forever.

In 1798 Mississippi became a territory of the new United States. On December 10, 1817, Mississippi became the 20th state to join the nation.

In the late 1700s and early 1800s, white settlers from more crowded states in the east began to move to Mississippi. They wanted to farm Mississippi's rich land. Neither the settlers nor the U.S. government cared that the land was already home to thousands of American Indians. The U.S. government thought it had a right to the land. The government forced the Choctaw and the Chickasaw to sign **treaties.** By signing these documents, the two nations agreed to give up all their land in the state of Mississippi.

When Mississippi became a U.S. territory, Natchez, an important river town, was its capital.

During the 1830s, the U.S. Army forced most of the Choctaw and the Chickasaw to leave Mississippi. The Indians were sent to Oklahoma, which was then called Indian Territory.

The Choctaw and the Chickasaw Indians were forced to leave their homelands in Mississippi during the 1830s. They walked along the Trail of Tears to what later became Oklahoma.

During the long march west to Indian territory, thousands of Indians died from disease, thirst, and hunger. Because of all the suffering, this forced march is called the Trail of Tears.

During the next 30 years, some of Mississippi's white settlers grew quite rich by growing cotton on large farms. These farms were called **plantations.** Black people—who had been brought to America from Africa as slaves—were forced to do the back-breaking work of planting and harvesting. By 1860 black slaves made up more than half of Mississippi's population.

The Devil's Backbone

One of Mississippi's most important highways was the Natchez Trace, an overland route stretching nearly 500 miles from Natchez, Mississippi, to Nashville, Tennessee. Herds of buffalo originally beat the path through the woods thousands of years ago. For many years, Indians in central Tennessee used the trail to get to the Mississippi River, where they traded with other Indians. In the late 1700s and early 1800s, white settlers from the east followed the ancient overland route to Mississippi. White traders used the trail, too. Starting in 1800, the U.S. government began using the Natchez Trace as the postal route to Mississippi and Louisiana.

But the trail was dangerous. Along the way, a traveler had to walk through dense forests in all kinds of weather. Travelers sometimes had to wade through swamps and swim across rivers. Wild animals and poisonous snakes were common. So were fierce outlaws who waited to rob or even kill travelers. Because of these hazards, the Natchez Trace became known as the Devil's Backbone.

In the early 1820s, travelers deserted the Natchez Trace in favor of steamboats, which could safely travel the mighty Mississippi River. In 1938 the U.S. government established the Natchez Trace Parkway, a road that follows the old trail. The National Park Service maintains the road and the many historic sites along the way. In this way, the Devil's Backbone will be preserved for generations to come.

A sign points hikers in the direction of the old Natchez Trace.

Many of the biggest plantations were close to the Mississippi River. Cotton grew well in the rich soil along the banks of the river. Plantation owners could easily load their harvests onto steamboats, which carried the crop to market. Prices for cotton were high, and Mississippi became one of the richest states in the country.

Many Northerners did not approve of using slave

Big bales of cotton were brought to Mississippi River docks. Steamboats carried the cotton north to be made into cloth.

labor. The Northern states had outlawed slavery, and many Northerners wanted Southern states to do the same. Southerners protested. They worried that their farms and plantations would not succeed without slave labor.

To protect the interests of their state, Mississippians left the Union (the United States) in 1861. They joined other Southern states to form the Confederate States of America, also called the Confederacy.

In February 1861, Jefferson Davis, a planter and U.S. senator from Mississippi, became president of the Confederacy. Just two months later, the Civil War broke out between the Northern and Southern states. About 80,000 Mississippians fought for the Confederacy during this bloody war.

When the Southern states formed their own nation, the Confederate States of America, Jefferson Davis became its president.

The state was the site of 16 major Civil War battles and hundreds of smaller conflicts. The most important battle there was fought in 1863 at Vicksburg.

For 47 days, the Northern army attacked the city, hoping to gain control of this important river town. To escape the attack, residents hid in hillside caves, which were crowded and filled with mosquitoes. With little food and few supplies, the Southern army had to give up. The battle was a major turning point in the Civil War.

Almost two years later, the North finally won the war. Afterward, Mississippians went through a difficult period called **Reconstruction.** During this time, Mississippi residents rebuilt their state. Their houses, barns, railroads, crops, and livestock had been destroyed during the war. Most people were very poor.

African Americans had been freed from slavery during the war. During Reconstruction, the U.S. government allowed Mississippi and other Southern states to rejoin the Union, but only after they had granted new rights to African Americans. Mississippi agreed to give black men the right to vote and hold political office. In 1870 Mississippi was readmitted to the Union.

Union soldiers lived in these temporary shelters during the 47-day siege of Vicksburg.

But many white people in Mississippi did not want black people to have the same rights as whites. Some whites joined the Ku Klux Klan, a violent group that threatened and killed black people. Klan members hoped that their actions would scare African Americans and keep them from standing up for their rights.

Cotton was still one of Mississippi's most important crops during the late 1800s.

In 1890 Mississippi passed new laws preventing blacks from exercising their right to vote. Other laws said that blacks were not allowed to attend the same schools as whites. They couldn't use the same bathrooms, hotel rooms, restaurants, schools, or drinking fountains. Without the freedom to vote, black Mississippians could not change the unfair laws.

Mississippi farmers continued to grow cotton after the war. Plantation owners could no longer use slaves, so they turned instead to **sharecroppers**. These were laborers who worked a small piece of land on a plantation. Plantation owners gave the sharecroppers seeds and tools.

After the harvest, sharecroppers had to give most of their crops to the plantation owners. Sharecroppers were left with very little of their own. They struggled to make a living.

By the beginning of the 1900s, many Mississippians were very poor. Farmers earned most of their money from cotton, but prices for the crop fell to low levels.

To make matters worse, the Great Depression hit the United States in 1929. Many farms, banks, and other businesses closed. During the 1930s, many people left Mississippi to look for better jobs.

Simple cabins like this one provided homes for many rural Mississippians.

In 1936, to help bring new jobs and more money to the state, Mississippi's government started a program to help build factories. Thousands of new jobs were created, many of them in shipbuilding. The discovery of oil at Tinsley in 1939 provided even more new jobs.

During World War II (1939–1945), factories near Flora and Aberdeen began producing weapons. Shipbuilding boomed in Pascagoula. The U.S. government also opened military training camps and airfields throughout the state. All this activity helped boost the state's economy.

The defense industry grew in Mississippi during World War II. Many women took jobs in defense plants.

After the war, African Americans in Mississippi and other Southern states began a new fight for equal rights. This fight was called the **civil rights movement**. In 1954 the U.S. Supreme Court ruled that black students and white students should be allowed to attend the same public schools.

Eight years later, in 1962, a black Mississippian named James Meredith tried to enroll at the all-white University of Mississippi. A large group of white people gathered to protest. Violence broke out, and two people were killed. Meredith enrolled, but U.S. government troops stayed at the university to protect him from angry whites until he graduated in 1963.

One year later, civil rights activist Fannie Lou Hamer established the Mississippi Freedom Democratic Party (MFDP), a racially mixed alternative to the all-white Mississippi Democratic Party.

James Meredith was the first black student to enroll at the University of Mississippi.

Hamer also spoke during the 1964 Democratic National Convention about the struggles of black people in the United States.

In 1965 the federal government passed the Voting Rights Act. This law removed restrictions that had kept black Mississippians from voting in elections. Many African Americans in Mississippi voted for the first time in their lives. In 1969 the citizens of Fayette elected Charles Evers—the first black mayor in Mississippi since Reconstruction.

Civil rights marchers greet field workers in Mississippi.

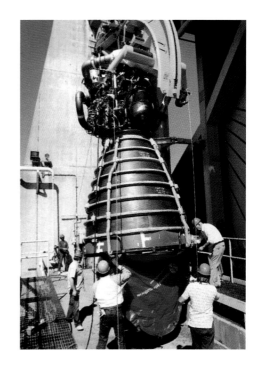

Workers at the John C. Stennis Space Center position a space-shuttle engine on a special stand for testing.

By the mid-1960s, more Mississippians were working in factories than on farms. But many of these factory jobs paid low wages. Compared to other states, Mississippi was poor. Mississippi leaders looked for new ways to improve the state's economy.

One important new business was the John C. Stennis Space Center, which opened in Hancock County in the 1960s. Operated by the National Aeronautics and Space Administration (NASA), the center helps build and test equipment for the U.S. space program. It also provides many jobs for Mississippi residents.

Another big facility, the Tennessee-Tombigbee Waterway, opened in 1985. The waterway gives the state's industries a quick and inexpensive route for shipping goods to ports on the Gulf of Mexico. The project has also brought many new jobs to the state.

In 1990 the state legislature legalized dockside casino gambling in Mississippi. By 2001 more than 25 casinos were operating in the state. These casinos, which feature gambling, dining, and entertainment, not only attract tourists to Mississippi but also provide many jobs for Mississippians. One casino, the

The Tennessee-Tombigbee Waterway is an important shipping route in eastern Mississippi.

This casino is on a boat docked in Biloxi, Mississippi.

Silver Star, is operated by the Mississippi Band of Choctaw Indians.

Mississippians celebrated in November 2000 when the Nissan Motor Company announced that it would build a big auto assembly plant near Jackson, just south of the city of Canton. The factory is expected to produce 250,000 pickup trucks a year and employ 4,000 workers. Construction on the factory began in 2001 and is set to end in 2003. Projects like this make Mississippians proud of their state and hopeful for its future.

PEOPLE & ECONOMY

The State of Change

ative Americans and pioneers once made their way to Mississippi by traveling along a path called the Natchez Trace or by boating down the Mississippi River. The first settlers lived in villages, on farms, or in small towns. In modern days, airports and highways link Mississippi to the rest of the country, and the state's cities and industries are growing. For this reason, many Mississippians call their state the State of Change.

Mississippi is home to about 2.8 million people. About 60 percent of the state's residents are white people. The ancestors of most Mississippians came to the United States from Great Britain, France, and other European countries.

Mississippians enjoy music and food at an outdoor blues festival.

About one out of every three Mississippi residents is African American. Almost all black Mississippians were born in the United States and can trace their roots back to Africa. Asian Americans, Latinos, and American Indians together make up about 3 percent of the population.

When the U.S. government moved Indians west in the 1830s, about 5,000 Choctaw Indians refused to leave their homeland in Mississippi. Some of their descendants live on the Choctaw Reservation, land in east-central Mississippi that the government reserved, or set aside, for these Indians. Nearby is Nanih Waiya, a mound that the Choctaw believe to be the birthplace of their people.

Almost half of Mississippi's residents live in cities. Many Mississippians who live in rural areas drive to work in nearby cities. Mississippi's largest cities are Jackson (the state capital), Gulfport, Biloxi, Hattiesburg, Greenville, and Meridian.

A Choctaw girl wears colorful beadwork.

Mississippi's capitol building in Jackson

Communities throughout Mississippi host many festivals during the year. The Choctaw celebrate their heritage at the Choctaw Indian Fair, held each July in Philadelphia, Mississippi. In nearby Jackson, the State Fair draws many people in fall, as does the Sweet Potato Festival in Vardaman.

Biloxi holds a shrimp festival each June to celebrate the beginning of the shrimp-fishing season.

Townspeople crown a shrimp queen and bless the fishing boats.

Visitors to Mississippi find many different kinds of music in the state. One of the most popular musical events is the Mississippi Delta Blues and Heritage Festival, held each fall in Greenville. In the spring, fans of country music enjoy performances by country-western singers at the Jimmie Rodgers Festival in Meridian.

With its mild climate, Mississippi is a great place to be outdoors. Miles of white, sandy beaches attract sunbathers to the Gulf Coast year-round.

Summertime activities in Mississippi include hot-air balloon races *(above)* and waterskiing *(right)*.

Longwood is a grand mansion in Natchez that was built before the Civil War.

The Tennessee-Tombigbee Waterway is a good place for boating and waterskiing. And many people enjoy hiking the nature trails along the Natchez Trace Parkway.

History buffs can try to imagine what life was like before the Civil War at plantations in Vicksburg, Natchez, and Columbus. Guides dressed in clothes in the style of the 1800s lead tours through these big farms and homes. At Florewood River Plantation near Greenwood, visitors can also see how crops were planted and harvested in the 1800s.

Those who want to learn more about Native American history can visit Grand Village of the Natchez Indians, a model of a Natchez village.

Nearby is Emerald Mound. Built about 1,000 years ago by mound-building Indians, Emerald is the third largest mound in the United States. Winterville Mounds in Greenville is home to more mounds than almost any other area of the Mississippi River valley.

Many Mississippians help tourists enjoy vacations in the state. These workers, including hotel clerks and chefs, have what are called service jobs. In fact, more than half of all working Mississippians have some kind of service job. Service workers are employed as bank tellers, nurses, lawyers, and salespeople, among many other kinds of jobs.

A service worker takes visitors on a tour of a historic neighborhood in Natchez.

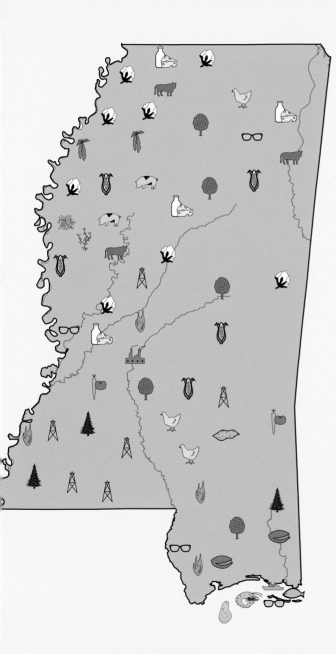

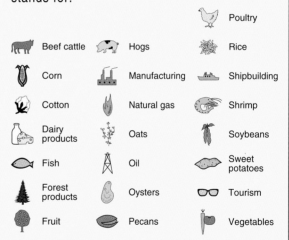

MISSISSIPPI
Economic Map

The symbols on this map show where different economic activities take place in Mississippi. The legend below explains what each symbol stands for.

	Beef cattle		Hogs		Poultry
	Corn		Manufacturing		Rice
	Cotton		Natural gas		Shipbuilding
	Dairy products		Oats		Shrimp
	Fish		Oil		Soybeans
	Forest products		Oysters		Sweet potatoes
	Fruit		Pecans		Tourism
					Vegetables

49

About one out of every five working people in Mississippi has a manufacturing job. Some manufacturers make plywood, paper products, boxes, and furniture out of lumber from the state's forests. Other manufacturers make stereos, telephones, chemicals, plastics, and clothing. Workers also package meat and shrimp at food processing plants. Pascagoula is still an important center for shipbuilding.

Agriculture is no longer as important as it once was in Mississippi. But farmers still grow cotton, and soybeans are also a major crop. Pecans, sweet

Workers pick cotton on a modern Mississippi farm.

potatoes, cucumbers, peaches, watermelons, and grapes are also grown in Mississippi. Many farmers raise chickens and beef and dairy cattle.

Very few of Mississippi's workers—only 1 percent—have jobs in mining. Miners dig for limestone, clay, and sand and gravel. Others look for petroleum and natural gas.

Mississippi earns millions of dollars from fishing. Shrimp is the most important catch, but fishers also bring in oysters, red snapper, and menhaden. And Mississippi's fish farmers raise more catfish each year than any other state in the country.

The Gulf of Mexico provides many jobs. Some people drill for oil at huge offshore platforms *(above left)*, while others catch shrimp in the gulf *(above right)*.

The Dangers of Dioxin

With more than 17 million acres of forest-land, wood is one of Mississippi's most important natural resources. Many people in the state earn a living by chopping down trees, working in sawmills, or making wood products such as furniture and paper.

Some people burn wood for heat and cooking, at home and on camping trips. But burning wood and manufacturing some wood products can produce a dangerous chemical called **dioxin**, which is harmful to the environment. Fireplaces, wood-burning stoves, and forest fires can all emit dioxin. Garbage-burning plants and factories that make chemicals that kill insects and weeds also produce dioxin. The main source of dioxin in Mississippi is paper mills.

Forests cover millions of acres of Mississippi's land *(above)*. Lumber companies use big machines to cut down and transport the lumber *(inset)*.

Logs are stored in large stacks before they are used to make paper.

Paper mills make paper by cutting up logs into chips. The chips are then mixed with chemicals and cooked at high temperatures to produce pulp, a soft, woody material. The pulp is washed and then bleached with chlorine, which makes the paper white and long-lasting. Dioxin is produced during the bleaching process—when wood, chlorine, and heat are combined.

After bleaching, the wet pulp is spread out on large screens and passed between rollers, which squeeze out all the water. Every year, paper mills produce millions of gallons of this

wastewater, which is contaminated with dioxin. Water treatment plants in cities and towns are unable to handle so much wastewater. So mill operators must apply for government permits, allowing them to empty their wastewater into nearby rivers and streams. The government tries to limit the amount of dioxin that can be emptied into waterways, but the chemical still ends up in the state's rivers and streams.

At this paper mill, lumber is ground into paper products such as towels, tissues, and paper.

When dioxin enters the waterways, it pollutes not only the water but also the plants and animals that live in the water. Fish become contaminated from eating the poisoned plants. Over time, fish build up a lot of dioxin in their bodies.

Scientists have found that dioxin causes birth defects and cancer in animals. The U.S. Environmental Protection Agency (EPA) believes that dioxin can cause cancer in human beings, too.

Over the years, Mississippi has performed a series of tests to measure dioxin in the state's rivers and fish. Researchers in southeastern Mississippi discovered that the amount of dioxin in certain fish was above the level that the EPA thought was safe.

Fish can absorb dioxin into their bodies.

Signs warn people of the dangers of eating fish from rivers that contain dioxin.

After the tests, Mississippi's leaders worried that people who regularly ate fish from the state's rivers might develop cancer.

Because of these studies, Mississippi urged people not to eat any fish from a river that tested high in dioxin. People were also warned to eat only small fish and to avoid larger, older fish, which might have a lot of dioxin in their bodies.

Mississippi began to try to reduce dioxin levels.

Some mills tried new methods of bleaching pulp that don't produce as much dioxin. The government also passed new laws reducing the amounts of dioxin that could be released into waterways.

The new methods and rules are very expensive, but the extra expense has paid off. In the late 1990s, scientists found that dioxin had dropped to safe levels in several state fishing areas. Warning signs were removed from these areas.

But the state remains cautious. Researchers are still studying the levels of dioxin in the state's waterways. Signs along contaminated rivers still warn people that the fish they catch could be harmful to their health. These steps will help protect residents and the environment. Looking for ways to reduce and prevent dioxin pollution is an important goal for Mississippians.

Keeping lakes and rivers clean is important to the people of Mississippi.

Fun Facts

Coca-Cola was first bottled in 1894 in Vicksburg, Mississippi. Joseph A. Biedenharn of the Biedenharn Candy Company poured the popular beverage into bottles so it could be delivered to rural, or country, areas that didn't have their own soda fountains.

Elvis Presley, a singer who became famous as the King of Rock and Roll, was born in Tupelo, Mississippi, on January 8, 1935.

In 1889 John L. Sullivan defeated Jake Kilrain near Hattiesburg, Mississippi, in the last world heavyweight bareknuckle boxing championship. The fight lasted 75 rounds.

More upholstered (padded and covered) furniture comes from Mississippi than from any other state in the country.

Coca-Cola was bottled for the first time at this company in Vicksburg.

Mississippi's state bird, the mockingbird, is a copycat. The small gray bird imitates all sorts of noises, from the sound of pianos to barking dogs.

Mississippi is sometimes called the Mud-Cat State for the many catfish that feed near the muddy bottoms of the state's waterways.

In 1902, on a hunting trip in Mississippi, President Theodore (Teddy) Roosevelt refused to shoot a bear. This event, drawn by a cartoonist, led to the creation of teddy bears.

Dr. James D. Hardy performed the world's first human heart transplant at Jackson's University of Mississippi Medical Center in 1964. Dr. Hardy replaced a sick human heart with the heart of a healthy chimpanzee.

The International Checkers Hall of Fame is located in Petal, Mississippi.

STATE SONG

Mississippi's state song was adopted in 1962.

GO, MISSISSIPPI

Words and music by Houston Davis

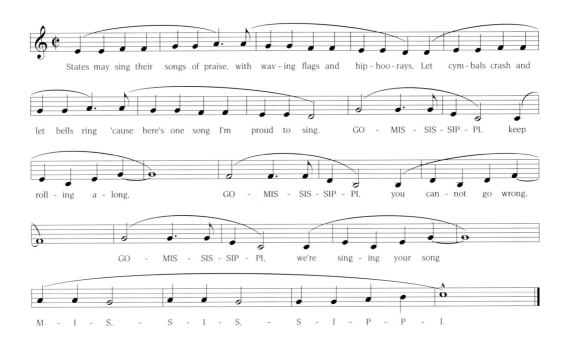

States may sing their songs of praise, with wav-ing flags and hip-hoo-rays, Let cym-bals crash and

let bells ring 'cause here's one song I'm proud to sing. GO - MIS - SIS - SIP - PI, keep

roll - ing a - long, GO - MIS - SIS - SIP - PI, you can-not go wrong,

GO - MIS - SIS - SIP - PI, we're sing-ing your song

M - I - S, - S - I - S, - S - I - P - P - I.

You can hear "Go, Mississippi" by visiting this website:
<http://www.50states.com/songs/miss.htm>

A MISSISSIPPI RECIPE

The mucky soil of the Mississippi River Delta is often called Mississippi Mud. That's also the name of a rich dessert featuring lots of chocolate, butterscotch, and gooey marshmallows.

MISSISSIPPI MUD BROWNIES

1 cup butterscotch chips
½ cup butter
1½ cups all-purpose flour
⅔ cup packed brown sugar
2 teaspoons baking powder

½ teaspoon salt
1 teaspoon vanilla extract
2 eggs
2 cups miniature marshmallows
2 cups chocolate chips

1. Ask an adult to preheat oven to 350° F.
2. Lightly grease a 9-inch by 13-inch baking pan.
3. With an adult's help, melt butterscotch chips and butter in a large bowl in a microwave oven.
4. Stir the mixture well and let it cool to lukewarm.
5. Mix flour, brown sugar, baking powder, and salt. Add vanilla and eggs, and add into the warm butterscotch mixture; mix well.
6. Fold in marshmallows and chocolate chips.
7. Spread batter into the greased baking pan.
8. Bake 25 minutes. Be sure not to overcook.

Makes 24 brownies.

HISTORICAL TIMELINE

18,000 B.C. Ancient hunters come to North America from Asia.

A.D. 700 Mound builders live in the region later called Mississippi.

1540s Between 25,000 and 35,000 Indians live in the Mississippi region.

1541 Hernando de Soto explores northern Mississippi.

1682 René-Robert Cavelier de La Salle claims the Mississippi River valley for France.

1699 Pierre Le Moyne establishes a French settlement at Old Biloxi.

1719 The first African slaves are brought to Mississippi.

1729 Natchez Indians revolt against French colonists.

1763 The British take control of the Mississippi region.

1798 Mississippi becomes a U.S. territory.

1817 Mississippi becomes the 20th state to join the Union.

1830s Choctaw and Chickasaw Indians are forced to leave Mississippi.

1861 Mississippi withdraws from the Union; the Civil War begins.

1863 Union troops defeat the Confederates at the Battle of Vicksburg.

1865 The Civil War ends in a Union victory.

1890 Mississippi passes new laws restricting the rights of African Americans.

1936 The Balancing Agriculture with Industry program helps bring new factories to Mississippi.

1939 Oil is discovered at Tinsley.

1962 James Meredith enrolls at the University of Mississippi.

1964 Fannie Lou Hamer establishes the Mississippi Freedom Democratic Party.

1985 The Tennessee-Tombigbee Waterway opens.

1990 Mississippi lawmakers allow dockside casino gambling.

2000 The Nissan Motor Company chooses a site near Canton for a new auto assembly plant.

OUTSTANDING MISSISSIPPIANS

Charles Evers

Medgar Evers

William Faulkner

Brett Favre

Craig Claiborne (1920–2000), born in Sunflower, Mississippi, served as the food editor for *The New York Times* for almost 30 years. He also wrote restaurant reviews and cookbooks, including *The New York Times Cook Book*, first published in 1961.

Charles Evers (born 1922) and **Medgar Evers** (1925–1963) were born in Decatur, Mississippi. The brothers were leaders in the civil rights movement in Mississippi. In 1963 Medgar was shot and killed. His murderer, a racist white man, was not convicted until 1994. In 1969 Charles became mayor of Fayette, Mississippi. The first black mayor in Mississippi since Reconstruction, he served four terms.

William Faulkner (1897–1962) lived most of his life in Oxford, Mississippi. The author wrote many short stories and novels, including *The Sound and the Fury* and *As I Lay Dying*. In 1949 Faulkner won the Nobel Prize for literature. He also won Pulitzer Prizes in 1955 and 1963.

Brett Favre (born 1969), a native of Gulfport, is one of the leading quarterbacks in the National Football League. He led the Green Bay Packers to victory in the 1997 Super Bowl. He was named the NFL's Most Valuable Player in 1995, 1996, and 1997.

Shelby Foote (born 1916), a prominent writer, was born in Greenville, Mississippi. He has written novels, history books, and literary criticism. His most famous work is *The Civil War: A Narrative*, a three-volume series.

Fannie Lou Hamer (1917–1977) was a leading civil rights activist. She grew up in a sharecropper family with 20 children. She went on to found the Mississippi Freedom Democratic Party and to speak at the 1964 Democratic National Convention.

Jim Henson

Jim Henson (1936–1990) of Greenville created a collection of puppets known as the Muppets. In 1955 Henson made his first puppet, Kermit the Frog, using his mother's old spring coat and a Ping-Pong ball. Henson later made Big Bird, the Cookie Monster, and other characters for the television show *Sesame Street*.

John Lee Hooker

John Lee Hooker (1917–2001) was a blues singer, songwriter, and guitar player from Clarksdale, Mississippi. He began his musical career in Detroit and later moved to Chicago. Hooker collaborated with many blues and rock performers over his long career. He is considered a legend among blues musicians.

James Earl Jones (born 1931) is an actor from Arkabutla, Mississippi. Known for his clear, deep voice, Jones provided the voice for Darth Vader in the *Star Wars* films. He has also appeared in many films and plays, and he won Tony Awards for his performances in the plays *The Great White Hope* and *Fences*.

James Earl Jones

B. B. King (born 1925) is from Indianola, Mississippi. One of the best-known blues musicians of all time, King sings and plays the guitar and clarinet. King's first initials come from an old stage name, the Blues Boy.

Trent Lott (born 1941) is a U.S. senator representing Mississippi. Lott was born in Grenada County, Mississippi. He was elected to the House of Representatives in 1972 and to the U.S. Senate in 1988. He served as the Senate's majority leader from 1996 to June 2001.

B.B. King

Muddy Waters

Walter Payton

Leontyne Price

LeeAnn Rimes

McKinley ("Muddy Waters") Morganfield (1915–1983) was a well-known blues singer from Rolling Fork, Mississippi. He also played the guitar and the harmonica. Morganfield's grandmother gave him his nickname, because as a boy he liked to play in a local creek.

Walter Payton (1954–1999) set the NFL record for rushing in a career, with a total of almost 17,000 yards in 13 seasons. The running back for the Chicago Bears was the NFL's Most Valuable Player in 1977 and 1985. He was born in Columbia, Mississippi.

Robert Pittman (born 1953) created MTV, a cable TV music network, in 1981. Since then, MTV has grown into a multimedia station, offering TV shows, music videos, Internet music downloads, Internet radio, and more. Pittman later worked as an executive at AOL Time Warner. He was born in Jackson.

Elvis Presley (1935–1977) is called the King of Rock and Roll. Born in Tupelo, Presley moved to Memphis as a teenager. His early hits include "Heartbreak Hotel," "Blue Suede Shoes," and "Hound Dog." Presley also acted in many movies. Graceland, his home in Memphis, is an international tourist attraction.

Leontyne Price (born 1927), an opera singer from Laurel, Mississippi, has starred in operas all over the world. The famous soprano has performed at the White House, at presidential inaugurations, and even for the pope. Price has won 20 Grammy Awards.

LeeAnn Rimes (born 1982) is one of country music's biggest stars. Born in Jackson, Rimes made her stage debut at age 7. She recorded her first major album, *Blue*, when she was just 14. Rimes has won many honors, including Grammy Awards, Academy of Country Music Awards, and Billboard Music Awards.

Ida B. Wells-Barnett (1862–1931) was a reporter and reformer who fought to protect blacks from violence. Born in Holly Springs, Mississippi, she moved to Memphis and then to Chicago. She also helped found the National Association for the Advancement of Colored People.

Eudora Welty

Eudora Welty (1909–2001) was a writer of short stories, novels, essays, and reviews. Much of her work dealt with small-town life in the South. In 1973 Welty won a Pulitzer Prize for her novel *The Optimist's Daughter*. Welty was born in Jackson.

Tennessee Williams (1911–1983), born in Columbus, Mississippi, was a famous American playwright. He won Pulitzer Prizes for the classic plays *A Streetcar Named Desire* and *Cat on a Hot Tin Roof*, both of which were made into movies.

Oprah Winfrey

Oprah Winfrey (born 1954) is an actress, talk-show host, and businesswoman from Kosciusko, Mississippi. Her *Oprah Winfrey Show*, which began in 1985, is one of the most popular shows on television. Winfrey has starred in several films, including *The Color Purple*. She also produces *O, the Oprah Magazine*, and runs Harpo Productions, a film and TV studio.

Richard Wright

Richard Wright (1908–1960) was one of the country's leading authors. He is best known for his novels *Native Son* and *Black Boy*, which are about being black in the United States. He also wrote poetry and essays. Wright was born near Natchez.

Tammy Wynette

Tammy Wynette (1942–1998) was an award-winning country music singer. Her hits include "D-I-V-O-R-C-E" and "Stand by Your Man." Wynette was born in Itawamba County.

FACTS-AT-A-GLANCE

Nickname: Magnolia State

Song: "Go, Mississippi"

Motto: Virtute et Armis (By Valor and Arms)

Flower: magnolia

Tree: magnolia

Bird: mockingbird

Insect: honeybee

Fossil: prehistoric whale

Shell: oyster shell

Stone: petrified wood

Beverage: milk

Date and ranking of statehood: December 10, 1817, the 20th state

Capital: Jackson

Area: 46,914 square miles

Rank in area, nationwide: 31st

Average January temperature: 46° F

Average July temperature: 81° F

Mississippi's flag features bars of red, white, and blue, the colors of the United States, along with the Confederate battle flag, used by Southern states during the Civil War.

POPULATION GROWTH

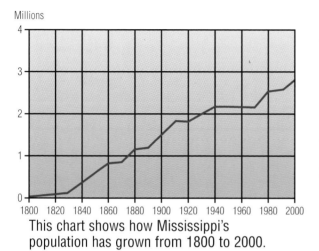

Millions

This chart shows how Mississippi's population has grown from 1800 to 2000.

The Mississippi state seal shows an eagle holding an olive branch and arrows. The olive branch symbolizes the desire for peace. The arrows show the ability to wage war if necessary.

Population: 2,844,658 (2000 census)

Rank in population, nationwide: 31st

Major cities and populations: (2000 census) Jackson (184,256), Gulfport (71,127), Biloxi (50,644), Hattiesburg (44,779), Greenville (41,633)

U.S. senators: 2

U.S. representatives: 4

Electoral votes: 6

Natural resources: bauxite, clay, iron ore, limestone, natural gas, petroleum, salt, sand and gravel, soil, trees, water

Agricultural products: beef cattle, chickens, cotton, cucumbers, dairy cattle, eggs, grapes, peaches, peanuts, pecans, rice, soybeans, sweet potatoes, watermelons, wheat

Fishing industry: buffalo fish, carp, catfish, menhaden, oysters, red snapper

Manufactured goods: chemicals, clothing, fertilizers, food products, furniture, lighting equipment, motor vehicle parts, paper products, plastics, ships, stereos, telephones, wood products

WHERE MISSISSIPPIANS WORK

Services—54 percent (services includes jobs in trade; community, social, and personal services; finance, insurance, and real estate; transportation, communication, and utilities)

Government—18 percent

Manufacturing—17 percent

Construction—5 percent

Agriculture—5 percent

Mining—1 percent

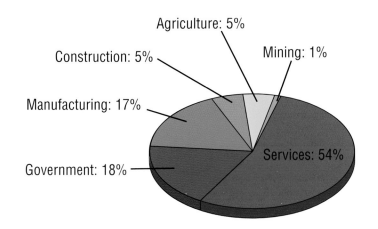

GROSS STATE PRODUCT

Services—54 percent

Manufacturing—22 percent

Government—15 percent

Construction—4 percent

Agriculture—4 percent

Mining—1 percent

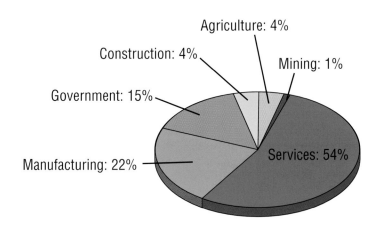

MISSISSIPPI WILDLIFE

Mammals: beaver, deer, fox, opossum, rabbit, squirrel

Birds: ducks, mockingbird, quail, turkey, wild dove

Amphibians and reptiles: alligator, frogs, lizards, salamanders, skink, snakes, toads, turtles

Fish: bass, bream, catfish, crab, crappie, mackerel, menhaden, oyster, red snapper, shrimp, speckled trout

Wild plants: azalea, black-eyed Susan, camellia, Cherokee roses, crepe myrtle, dogwood, redbud, violet, Virginia creeper

Trees: ash, bald cypress, cottonwood, elm, hickory, magnolia, oak, palm, pecan, pine, sweet gum, tupelo

A mallard duck

PLACES TO VISIT

Catfish Capitol, Belzoni

Exhibits teach about Mississippi's most famous fish—and one of its favorite foods. A video follows the catfish from fingerling to frying pan. A 40-foot catfish welcomes visitors outside.

Delta Blues Museum, Clarksdale

Visitors will learn about the history of blues music and about great Mississippi blues artists such as B. B. King, Muddy Waters, and John Lee Hooker.

Elvis Presley's Birthplace, Tupelo

The King of Rock and Roll was born here in 1935. The modest two-bedroom house in Tupelo draws 100,000 visitors annually.

Emerald Mound, Adams County

One of the largest ceremonial mounds in the United States, Emerald Mound rises 35 feet high and covers 8 acres. The surrounding area was home to ancestors of the Natchez Indians.

Florewood River Plantation, Greenwood

Learn about life on an 1850s cotton plantation. Attractions include a museum and reconstructed buildings such as a smokehouse, blacksmith shop, schoolhouse, and gristmill.

Grand Village of the Natchez Indians, Natchez

The 128-acre site features a museum, a reconstructed Natchez Indian house, and three ceremonial mounds, two of which have been excavated and rebuilt to their original appearance.

Mississippi Petrified Forest, Flora
The only petrified forest in the eastern United States, this park features giant ancient trees that long ago turned into stone, a nature trail, and an earth science museum.

Rowan Oak, Oxford
Rowan Oak was the home of famed Mississippi author William Faulkner. Visitors to the house can learn about the writer and his work.

StenniSphere, Stennis Space Center
Using displays, films, and interactive exhibits, StenniSphere teaches visitors about spacecraft and space exploration, the International Space Station, planet Earth, and the solar system.

Vicksburg National Military Park, Vicksburg
The Vicksburg battlefield site includes 1,325 historic monuments and markers, 20 miles of reconstructed trenches and earthworks, 144 cannons, the restored Union gunboat USS *Cairo*, the Vicksburg National Cemetery, and more.

The house where Elvis Presley was born draws thousands of fans each year.

ANNUAL EVENTS

Civil War Reenactment at Florewood River Plantation, Greenwood—*March*

Natchez Spring Pilgrimage, Natchez—*March–April*

Jimmie Rodgers Music Festival, Meridian—*May*

World Catfish Festival, Belzoni—*April*

Choctaw Indian Fair, Philadelphia—*July*

Watermelon Festival, Mize—*July*

Biloxi Seafood Festival, Biloxi—*September*

Mississippi Delta Blues and Heritage Festival, Greenville—*September*

Mississippi State Fair, Jackson—*October*

Tennessee Williams Festival, Clarksdale—*October*

National Sweet Potato Festival, Vardaman—*November*

LEARN MORE ABOUT MISSISSIPPI

BOOKS

General

George, Charles, and Linda George. *Mississippi*. Danbury, CT: Children's Press, 1999.

Shirley, David. *Mississippi*. New York: Benchmark Books, 1999.

Thompson, Kathleen. *Mississippi*. Austin, TX: Raintree Steck-Vaughn, 1996.

Special Interest

Bullard, Sara. *Free at Last: A History of the Civil Rights Movement and Those Who Died in the Struggle*. New York: Oxford University Press Children's Books, 1994. This book details the civil rights struggles of the 1950s and 1960s and profiles 40 people who lost their lives fighting for the cause. Several of them, including Medgar Evers, lived or worked in Mississippi.

Siebert, Diane. *Mississippi*. New York: HarperCollins Children's Books, 2001. Take a poetic journey through time on the Mississippi River. This story covers the region's history from its first Indian inhabitants to the modern era.

Welch, Catherine A. *Ida B. Wells-Barnett: Powerhouse with a Pen*. Minneapolis: Carolrhoda Books, Inc., 2000. Wells-Barnett was a reporter who fought to protect black Americans from violence and injustice. For older readers.

Fiction

Matas, Carol. *The War Within: A Novel of the Civil War*. New York: Simon & Schuster, 2001. The daughter of a successful merchant family in Mississippi, thirteen-year-old Hannah is like most other proper Southern girls—except her family is Jewish. When the Union Army orders all Jews to be evacuated from the territory, Hannah must reexamine her views on slavery and the Civil War.

Orcutt, Harrell. *Longwalker's Journey: A Novel of the Choctaw Trail of Tears*. New York: Dial Books for Young Readers, 1999. Drawing on her own family history, the author tells of the Choctaw Indians who were forced to leave eastern Mississippi in 1831. The book centers on ten-year-old Minko, who earns the name Longwalker during the journey.

Taylor, Mildred D. *Roll of Thunder, Hear My Cry*. New York: Phyllis Fogelman Books, 2001. This award-winning book records the struggle of the Logans, an African American family living in Mississippi in the 1930s. The story focuses on nine-year-old Cassie Logan as she learns difficult lessons about racism and injustice.

WEBSITES

The Official State Web Site of Mississippi
<http://www.ms.gov>
The official state website provides information on state government, education, business, and more. One section of the site offers lots of helpful material for visitors to Mississippi.

Mississippi Division of Tourism
<http://www.visitmississippi.org>
People planning a trip to Mississippi will find a wealth of useful information here, including details about historic attractions, special events, accommodations, restaurants, and recreation. The site includes a special kids' section.

The Clarion-Ledger
<http://www.clarionledger.com>
The Clarion-Ledger is published in Jackson, Mississippi's capital and biggest city. The paper provides news and information about the city itself and also covers important events in Mississippi, the United States, and the world.

PRONUNCIATION GUIDE

Biloxi (buh-LUHK-see)

Chickasaw (CHIHK-uh-saw)

Choctaw (CHAHK-taw)

de Soto, Hernando (dih SOH-toh, hehr-NAHN-doh)

Hattiesburg (HAT-eez-burg)

La Salle, René-Robert Cavelier de (luh SAL, ruh-NAY-roh-BEHR ka-vuhl-yay duh)

Meridian (muh-RIHD-ee-uhn)

Natchez (NACH-ehz)

Pascagoula (pas-kuh-GOO-luh)

Tombigbee (tahm-BIHG-bee)

Yazoo (ya-ZOO)

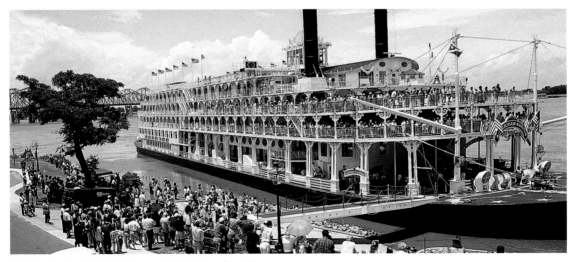

A Mississippi steamboat stops near Natchez.

GLOSSARY

alluvium: a mixture of clay, silt, sand, and gravel deposited by a river's running water. This mixture provides very good soil for farming.

civil rights movement: the movement to gain equal rights, or freedoms, for all citizens—regardless of race, religion, or sex

delta: A triangular piece of land at the mouth of a river. Deltas are formed from soil deposited by the river.

dioxin: a poisonous chemical that contains carbon, oxygen, and chlorine. Dioxin can kill some animals and cause health problems in humans.

plantation: a large farm that is also home to the farm owners and farm workers. In the past, American plantation owners often used slave labor.

prairie: a large area of level or gently rolling grassy land with few trees

Reconstruction: the period from 1865 to 1877, during which the U.S. government rebuilt Southern cities and businesses that had been destroyed during the Civil War. During this period, the government also determined how to bring the Southern states back into the Union.

sharecropping: a system in which laborers, called sharecroppers, work on a large farm in exchange for a share of the crops they produce

treaty: an agreement between two or more groups, usually having to do with peace or trade

INDEX

PHOTO ACKNOWLEDGMENTS